In the Club

For Nyrah, my own little sleep thief, who stole my heart as well as my Sunday lie-ins.

A STUDIO PRESS BOOK

First published in the UK in 2021 by Studio Press,
an imprint of Bonnier Books UK,
The Plaza, 535 King's Road, London SW10 0SZ
Owned by Bonnier Books,
Sveavägen 56, Stockholm, Sweden

www.bonnierbooks.co.uk

Text and illustrations copyright © 2021 Helene Weston

1 3 5 7 9 10 8 6 4 2

ISBN 978-1-80078-111-5

MIX
Paper from
responsible sources
FSC® C104723
FSC
www.fsc.org

Edited by Emma Drage
Designed by Nia Williams
Production by Emma Kidd

@helenetheillustrator

A CIP catalogue for this book is available from the British Library
Printed and bound in Poland

In the Club

A humorous guide for ^new mums

frazzled

STUDIO
PRESS

Perhaps you are pregnant, have just given birth, or are a frazzled new mum trying to navigate the first year of motherhood. Or maybe your little one is going through a phase that feels like it will never end and you feel overwhelmed and underqualified? Well, you're in good company!

Welcome to the club!

I hope you will find some comfort and solidarity in this book.

I was lucky enough to have a pretty uneventful pregnancy with my daughter. I met my new NCT friends for coffee and cake, made lists of stuff I knew I didn't really need, and tried to learn hypnobirthing ready for the drug-free water birth that I'd planned to have at our local midwife-led unit.

What actually happened was a gruelling three-day labour, ALL the drugs, an assisted birth, an infection, four days in hospital, a baby born with a medical condition... and me being left with bladder issues for around six weeks post-birth. Now who could have predicted that? Certainly not me. I had no idea any of that was even a possibility.

I'm sure our crappy start didn't help, but what followed was a massive shock for us both as new parents. My expectations were far from the reality I was experiencing.

I felt like I'd been completely conned. Why didn't anyone tell me this is how it would be?

For at least the first year of my daughter's life, I felt completely out of my depth and not like myself at all... What the fuck had we done?!

I would scroll through Instagram thinking, 'Who are these women giving this picture-perfect perception of being a new mum?' I'm sitting here with hideously sore nipples, a baby who never sleeps and a feeling of complete shock. Surely I can't be the only one not enjoying this?

I'm here to show new mums that they are not alone. They say it's the hardest job in the world but nobody tells you why. Nobody tells you that not everyone feels that rush of love at the start, or that sometimes you'll find being a new mum really lonely or struggle to adjust to your new life.

If you're reading this when you're pregnant, I really don't want it to scare you. You very well might get the birth you wanted and had planned, you might get a baby who sleeps and you might love every second of being a new mum, and that's ace.

No matter what shite you go through as a new parent, it goes without saying that it's all completely 100 million percent worth it. Being a mum is the best thing in the world and just gets better and better.

I know that all mums are different, all babies are different and all births are different, and that's why this book is judgement free. You do what you gotta do. We're all just making it up as we go along, hoping for the best, right?

So come on in! The tea is lukewarm and the conversations are unfinished, but we're all in this together!

Chapter 1
Early Days

"enjoy every minute!"

The Fourth Trimester

Nobody tells you about the Fourth Trimester. Almost as soon as you have given birth, you're practically on your own holding someone else's life literally in your hands. No pressure then.

Try not to feel bad if you're not enjoying every single second with your newborn. I didn't. Every day was survival.

Who actually 'enjoys' sleep deprivation, being continuously puked on, and walking like John Wayne for weeks with not so much as a smile of recognition in return?

If all you've done today is sit on the sofa and feed your baby, change shitty nappies and destroy a family-sized tin of biscuits… that's completely fine. I'm here to tell you that You Are Enough. Yes, you! Everyone finds this bit really bloody hard; some mums are just better at hiding it than others!

And it's totally okay to miss your old life – it doesn't mean you don't appreciate your new one.

What Now?

All new parents have that moment, either on the drive back from the hospital or when you first bring the baby into your home, when it hits you… 'What the hell do we do now?!'

Welcome to your new job. This little bundle of joy is your new boss.

Oh, and the hours are 24/7, there's no sick pay or annual leave, and the future happiness and wellbeing of the next generation depends on you.

Have fun but, whatever you do, don't mess it up!

As a first-time parent, you'll never quite know if you're doing it the right way and everyone you meet will tell you something different, but that's because all babies are different, and rest assured we are ALL making this up as we go along.

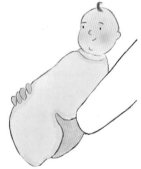

Here's your new job, don't fuck it up ~

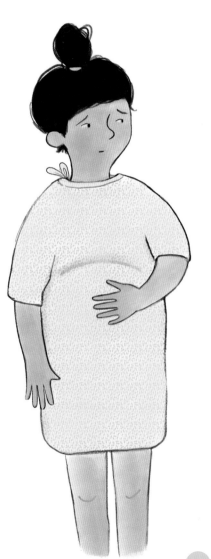

How I imagined
our first photo ↓

the reality ↓

The First Photo

When I imagined our first photo together, I pictured blissful looks, rosy cheeks and perhaps a bit of a sweaty brow…

In reality, I looked like I'd been run over, and then a vampire had stolen all of my blood… and punched me in the eyes… twice.

I was more exhausted than I'd ever been in my life but absolutely euphoric. I couldn't believe that my baby was actually here!

It may not be my finest Instaworthy photo but it speaks volumes.

There's a reason they call it labour!

You Did It!

No matter how you gave birth, you should be so, SO proud of yourself and your body... You bloody did it!

Maybe you got the birth you wanted or maybe you didn't.

You might have feelings about the birth you'll need to work through later, but right now enjoy that soggy hospital toast and stewed cup of tea. You are a goddess (albeit a bloated, sweaty, exhausted one).

Some mums feel that overwhelming surge of love, some don't — and that's okay, it doesn't mean you won't.

All I remember thinking was 'Thank fuck that's over, can I go to sleep now please?'

In these first few days, everyone always asks about the baby. Remember to look after yourself too. You've just been through a monumental thing and your body probably won't feel like your own for a while, so be kind to it.

One Day at a Time

Try to remember to take each day as it comes. After all, you're just getting to know each other and this is all so new for both of you.

Don't plan to do too much or put pressure on yourself to get the hang of being a mum straight away. You wouldn't expect to be able to take your driving test after just a couple of lessons, would you?

It can feel so overwhelming to be a new mum but, unless you tell your friends and family how you are feeling, nobody will know.

A newborn brings much excitement, and everyone will probably want to have a nosey, but remember you're allowed to set your own boundaries. If you don't feel comfortable with Uncle Bob popping over to gawp at the newest member of the family then tell him to bog off. (Or perhaps tell him to come back in a couple of weeks.)

This is your time as a brand-new family. You're allowed to be 'closed to visitors' for as long as you like, until you feel ready.

Magical Moments

Breathe in that delicious new-baby smell. Feel their softer-than-soft little head and tiny little fingers that wrap around yours. For amongst all the chaos, the mind-numbing sleep deprivation, the puke and the poo, there is this.

Enjoy these fleeting moments of calm when they are so content just to be near you, and you'll realise that being your baby's whole world actually feels pretty awesome.

PS After looking into the science (Dr Google) about 'why newborns smell so good', I discovered that nobody really knows, apart from a suggestion about bonding and vernix (barf) … Not sure how I feel about sniffing my friend's new baby now.

I'm convinced that midwives sprinkle some kind of magical hypnotising love potion on your baby's head when you're not looking.

The Newborn Bubble

No matter how long you've been planning for this, or how much you've wanted it, nothing can prepare you for the shock of having that small human in your life.

You'll stare at them for hours and hours on end, find them the most fascinating thing you've ever seen, and every little snuffle or tiny noise they make will make your heart leap.

You have your very own human pet to obsess over. You are now responsible for keeping this little bugger ALIVE and happy. It's a lot.

You will watch them breathe, worry about them and feel completely overwhelmed at times.

Relax into the newborn bubble where hazy days and nights blend into one, and hours disappear in the relentless cycle of feeding, bum changing, sleeping… and staring.

Small Wins

There will be days when having a shower feels like a massive achievement, when your baby won't want to be put down for a second, even to let you have a poo in peace.

Try not to compare yourself to other mums.

That mum who looks like she's got her shit together is probably just having a good day.

You'll have good days, you'll have bad days. You'll have days when you don't know how you'll make it out of the house, never mind get ready to face other mums at a baby group.

Plonk your bum on the sofa, open that massive tin of chocolate biscuits and drink that cold cup of tea you made 20 minutes ago. Tomorrow is a brand-new day.

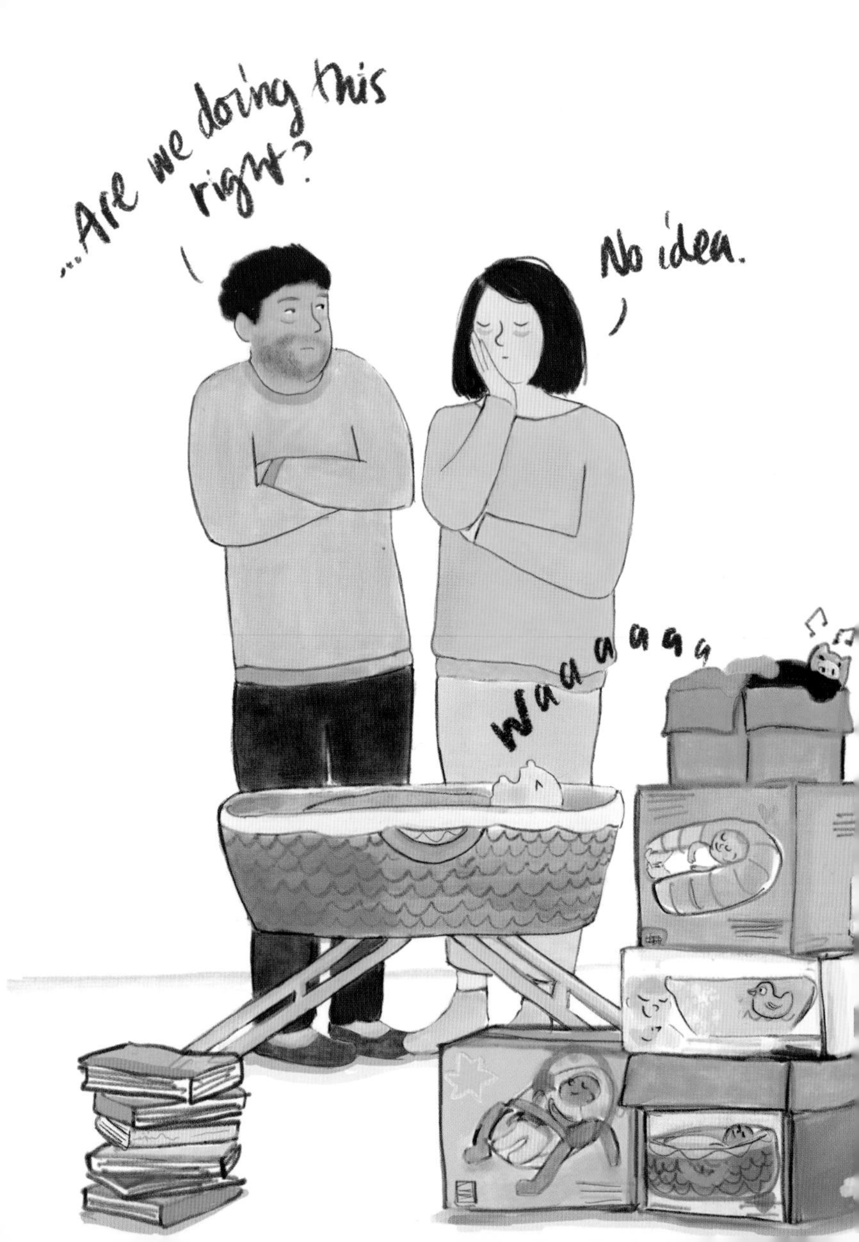
...Are we doing this right?
No idea.
Waaaaaaa

Are We Doing This Right?

Being a new parent can be overwhelming and, of course, it can be scary.

No matter what you do, there will be someone saying they 'wouldn't do it like that' or scaring you with stories that they read on an online forum or heard from their friend at NCT.

You have to learn to trust yourself. You know your baby best even if you don't believe it and feel completely underqualified, sleep deprived and exhausted.

If you have a partner, stick together, tag team, eat ALL the biscuits and give each other a break. (Even if they don't do the nappies up right and dress them in mismatched outfits, try not to murder each other.)

If you're doing this solo, don't be afraid to ask for help.

You'll get through this.

'Helpful' Advice

You cannot love a baby too much. No, you're not spoiling him, and, no, you're not making a rod for your own back.

You can let people give their advice, but at the end of the day they do not have a clue what your baby needs, just as much as you don't know their baby.

What works for one baby will not work for another – it's not one size fits all here. You'll discover that all babies are unique and all have their special little quirks. It's what makes us human.

You'll also discover that no sooner have you found a technique or method that works than your darling little poppet will decide they don't like that anymore and you'll be right back at square one.

Don't let 'well-wishers' make you feel like you're doing it wrong.

You do you. Smile and nod and mentally flip them the bird.

Oh I wouldn't carry him so much if I were you, you'll make a rod for your own back, blah blah blah...

She soon came to
realise that
EVERYONE

was finding this
really fucking hard

Everyone is Winging It

Some mums will make out they're fine when they're really not. The pressure of being a new parent and feeling judged by others can sometimes make you feel like a total failure before you've even started.

Leaving the house can feel like a HUGE ordeal. You may be worried that you won't be able to get your pram into the café, or that your baby will cry in public. You may feel anxious about trying to breastfeed without flashing your boobs to the world.

Try to remember that everyone is fighting their own battles and has their own shit going on. People just cope with things in different ways.

Who Even Am I?

For a long time after I had my baby, I didn't feel like myself. I couldn't put my finger on it, but I just felt 'different'.

Having a baby is a massive life change and the first few months can be a huge shock. Overnight your life changes completely: you can't just pop out to the shops or go away for the weekend anymore. You don't even have time to eat a meal or watch a movie uninterrupted.

Also, it sounds silly but none of my favourite clothes fitted, so I lived in maternity jeans for at least a year. (Okay, okay, I'm lying, it was two years. They're just so bloody comfy, alright?) Sometimes it was hard to make time to wash my hair, let alone make myself a healthy lunch and there was just no time for even a small amount of self-care (unless you count sitting in the car on the drive).

But slowly, slowly I came out of the fog and you will too. It takes a long time for some and others can just bounce back (damn them).

But… we're surviving!

Baby steps.

old me

New me

A Fed Baby is a Happy Baby

How you feed your baby is something that only you can decide. If you're happy and relaxed, it's more likely that your baby will be too.

Breastfeeding didn't work for some of my friends, but it worked for me. I was lucky. That's not to say it was easy. It wasn't. It hurt A LOT at the start, my nipples turned black, I had mastitis, I didn't feel confident, but I just carried on as I felt like that's what I was 'supposed' to be doing.

I said I was going to stop nearly every week, but in the end I loved it. It was the right thing for us and I was gutted when I had to stop due to going back on medication and returning to work when my daughter was eight months old.

Breastfeeding isn't right for everyone. Some want to feed but can't, some don't want to breastfeed – and that's okay. Some want to combine a bit of breastfeeding with a bit of bottle. Some adopt so don't have a choice. It's your own decision to make. I will say this though: whether it's with breastmilk or formula, there's nothing as cute as a milk-drunk baby. (Until they throw up on you, of course.)

Prepare for the Night Shift!

Prepare the bottles, the wipes, the soothers, shushers, rockers, puke mopper-uppers and matchsticks for your eyeballs!

Assemble all the things you can do with one hand. Get the boxset you're watching ready to go, the white noise app downloaded on your phone and the snacks at hand – this may be a long night.

If you always end up sleeping on the floor next to the cot, remember to drag in a spare mattress or at least a duvet. A sleep-deprived you will thank you for that in the wee small hours.

Don't forget to look into the eyes of that beautiful human you've created, and don't worry too much if you sprinkle biscuit crumbs on their little head – we all do that!

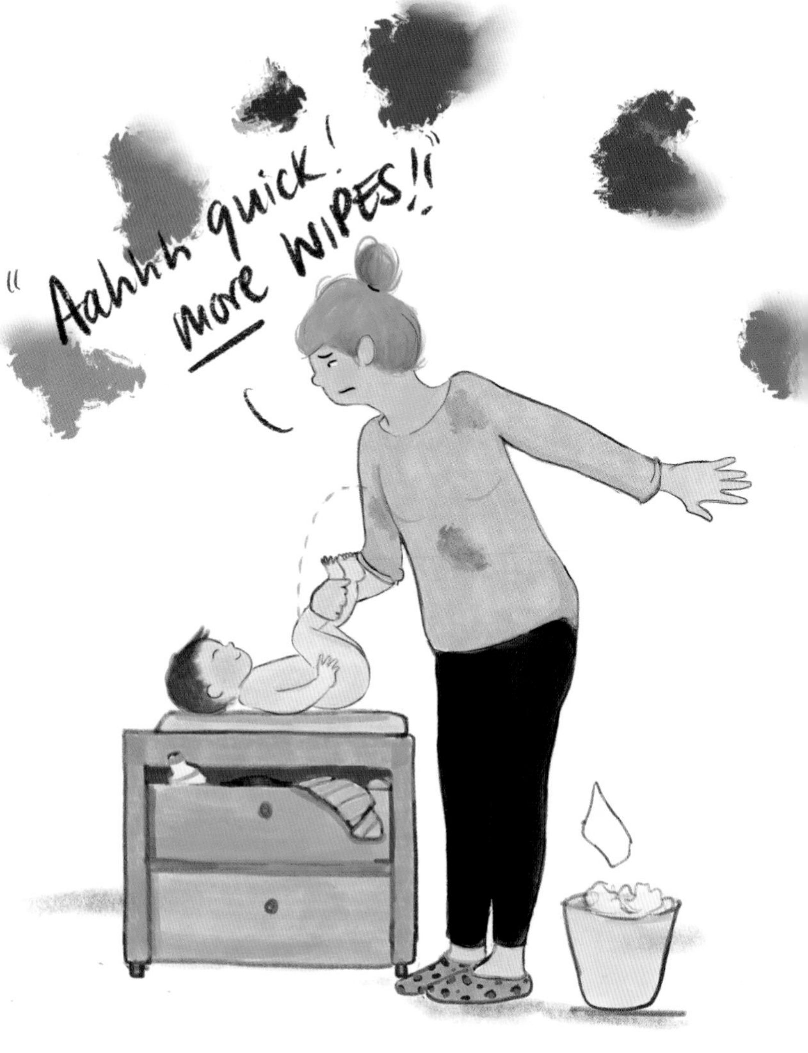
"Aahhh quick! more WIPES!!"

Nappy-changing Ninja

If, like me, you'd never changed a nappy before becoming a parent, it's pretty much a given that, to begin with, you'll make a right pig's ear of it. There will be stuff everywhere, you'll forget to have the wipes within reach and there will probably be poo on the carpet and piss in your eye.

But don't worry, within a couple of weeks you'll be an expert at this. You'll have everything set up in nappy changing 'stations' all over the house, you'll be able to smell a turd from 100 m. Work as a team, take it in turns, especially for a 'code brown'. That's true love right there.

Two TOP tricks:

1. Baby vests with envelope necks stretch so you can take them off by pulling them down. That way, you don't need to get the poor kid covered in turd by lifting it over his head.

2. Lay the clean nappy underneath the baby before removing the dirty one. This saves you from ferreting about finding a clean one with a hand full of crappy nappy – game changer.

Until… Pop! The Bubble Bursts

The first few weeks (months) of being a new mum are relentless. You've been riding high on adrenalin and then you suddenly feel like you've been hit by a double-decker bus.

I remember sobbing on the phone to my mum in the first few weeks that I couldn't do it, that I felt so out of my depth and just physically and mentally exhausted.

You'll cry A LOT and worry about things you never knew you could; I was terrified that I would drop her, that she would get ill and I wouldn't know what to do, that the room was too hot, or too cold.

With all the stress and hormones, being a new mum is an emotional rollercoaster. Rest assured that every first-time mum feels overwhelmed. For most, it's the hardest thing they've ever done.

You probably won't believe it, but you're doing so well and every day will feel a tiny little bit easier.

Brighter days are coming.

...I don't think I can do this, Mum...

Waaaaaa Waaaaaa!

Five Things You Might Need in the First Few Weeks

1. Someone to talk to

2. Boxsets

glug glug

nom nom nom

Binge time!

get cosy!

3. At least three family-sized tins of biscuits

4. Comfy PJs and the biggest pants you've ever worn

5. Just yourself – you can do this!

Chapter 2
Sleep - What's That?

Baby sleep guide!

No time to read

Happy Baby!

Sleep is for the Weak
(and People Without Kids)

In those first few months it's completely normal to become obsessed with exactly how many hours sleep you've both managed to have.

Days and nights will blend into one. People will tell you to 'sleep when the baby sleeps', which would be great if the baby actually slept in her cot and not only in the sodding car or while you are pounding the pavements with the pushchair.

The truth is that babies will wake you up all the time and that's completely normal. They think you're great! You're their favourite person and they want to spend every single second with you. They would probably crawl back inside you if they could! After all, they have been with you every single second for the past nine months.

Celebrate the monumentally small wins (they slept for a whole four hours!) and be kind to yourself.

Welcome to a New Level of Conversation

It feels great when you find a fellow member of the 'No Sleep Club'. You compare hours of the night like you're reading from a score sheet and they totally 'get' you. It's also a relief to realise you're not alone. You can guarantee that at 3 a.m. at least one member of your mums Whatsapp group will be awake too. Take solace in the fact that in the wee small hours of the morning there are mums (and dads) all over the planet doing exactly the same as you.

Sometimes, no words are needed. Your sleep-deprived brains can't even string a sentence together and that's okay. You both survived another night, and who knows what tonight will bring? Tonight might just be the night they sleep for more than two hours in one go! (But don't get your hopes up…)

The Cutest Assassin

For babies, cuteness is their superpower. One smile or giggle from them and you'll forgive the hours of screaming and broken sleep in an instant!

At times, the exhaustion of being a sleep-deprived parent can seem relentless. Pinching slithers of sleep like your life depends on it, night after night, can take its toll. Don't try to do it all yourself. Asking for help doesn't make you a failure. You're not a bloody robot and you can't pour from an empty sippy cup.

Every day, your baby is getting older and changing so much. The hard parts won't last and everything is temporary.

Apart from the love – that just grows and grows.

Just Sleep, Will You?

They're rubbing their eyes, yawning, grumbling…
it's definitely nap time. Ahh, the nap is king! An
hour or two to relax and have some 'you' time.

Or not.

Some babies have the power to fight sleep like
they're employed by MI5 and it's their one sole
mission to stay awake. Failure is not an option.
Must. Not. Sleep.

This is where you make that infamous 'rod for your
own back' and resort to driving around the block
for an hour. Make the most of your 'you time'.
Own that rod! Sit in the car and listen to a podcast,
go to the drive-through and get a hot chocolate,
park up and have a little nap yourself. Why not? You
deserve it.

If you're organised, you can pack a thermos and
some biscuits, synchronise naps with a mum pal and
park next to each other in a supermarket car park
for a natter… what a luxury!*

*Not even joking.

'Never Feed Your Baby to Sleep' and Other Really Unhelpful Advice You Read When You're Feeding Your Baby to Sleep

There will be lots of advice that people give you, albeit well-meaning. Ultimately, it's completely up to you to choose to take it, or ignore it.

If you want to feed your baby to sleep then that's up to you. Remember, you do you.

Don't fight battles with yourself because it says on the internet that it's not what you should be doing. Trust your own instincts.

For us, feeding to sleep was part of our routine. For others, it might not be right. We are all different… Did I mention that?

Party All Night

Once they come out into the brand-new big wide world, it understandably takes babies a while to adjust.

To a newborn baby, there's no such thing as night and day. Getting used to staying up all night can be bloody hard for new parents, especially if you're working in the day.

When you're trapped under a baby who will only sleep on you, try not to worry about all the things you could be getting done. You're doing the most important job in the world, right there! Sod the housework – that'll still be there tomorrow.

Babies have an in-built detector that goes off as soon as you even think about having a hot cup of tea, a wee or, heaven forbid, a shower.

Party hard all night, sleep all day – remember those days? Me neither.

Netflix and Chill

This is probably the only time you can get away with watching a whole series in a couple of days. Choose whatever you want: cheesy films your partner never wants to watch, reality TV on catch-up, documentaries on baboons… whatever floats your boat.

Probably nothing too taxing on the ole brain cells though. If you've always secretly fancied watching *The Housewives of Wimbledon,* this is your chance. (With only the little sleep thief to judge your terrible choices.) Make sure that you have everything you need within reach before you press play:

☐ Snacks

☐ Water

☐ Phone

☐ Tissues

If Looks Could Kill

Somehow, new mums have this built-in function that makes them wake up at the slightest noise from the baby. We can go from the deepest sleep to ★PING★ wide awake in an instant.

Some people could sleep though a tornado. That's all I'm saying.

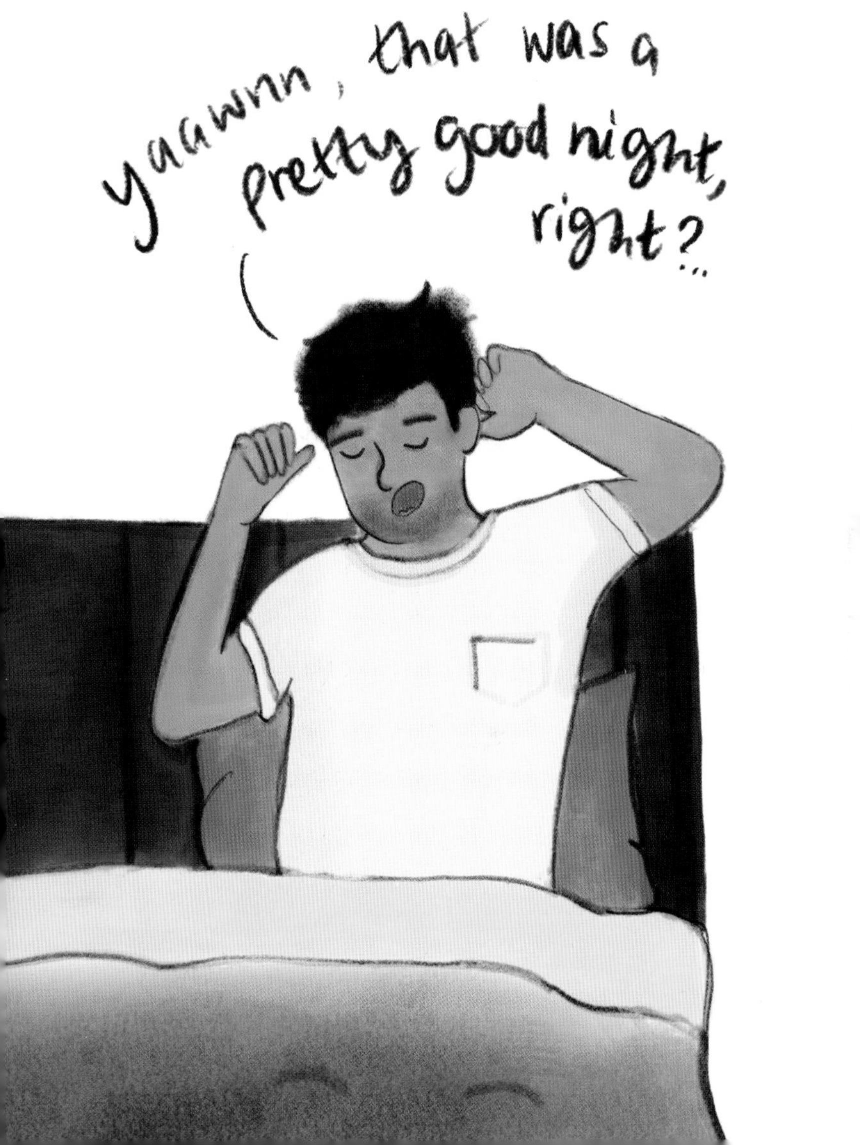
yaawnn, that was a pretty good night, right?...

Multitasking Like a Mother

Newborn snuggles are the best, like a cuddly little koala clinging onto you, keeping you warm and smelling of heaven… (Until you feel the rumble in the bottom jungle and a familiar pong drifts up towards your nostrils, of course.)

Make life easier for yourself and wear them in a sling. That way you'll have both hands free to make food, read a book (remember those?) or put the washing on.

Having a new little sidekick who will only sleep ON you, or with you rocking them and making weird humming and shhhing noises, can sometimes feel too much, but it won't last. Before you know it, they'll be telling you that 'you can go now, Mum'. ★weep★

You're So Annoying

In the depths of sleep deprivation, you'll both say things you don't mean, sometimes possibly really mean things. You'll argue about who is the most tired, or who has it easiest, who does the most, whose fucking idea this was…

You'll be insanely jealous if they get to leave the house to go to get more toilet roll from the shops and sob when they return to work, leaving you on your own with 'their' child.

Remember, this is tough for both of you. It's not their fault they don't have boobs or haven't mastered the one-handed nappy change yet.

Don't forget you're in this together. (And nine times out of ten the one who gave birth wins.)

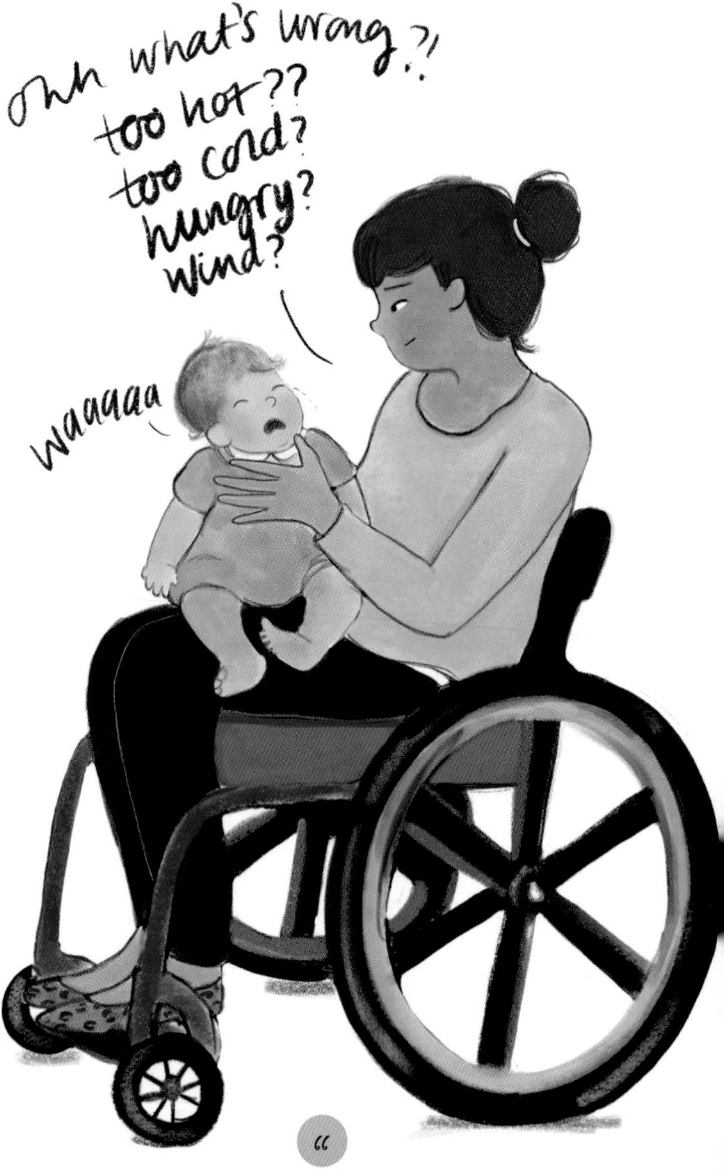
ohh what's wrong?!
too hot??
too cold?
hungry?
wind?
waaaaa

The Witching Hour(s)

Just when you think you've nearly made it through to the end of the day, 'The Witching Hour' is upon you, like a final punch in the guts before you even think about relaxing for a millisecond.

You're on your knees, dragging your ass past the finish line and suddenly a dark fog descends. In an instant, you become inept at knowing what your child needs… 'What do you want from me? Why isn't this working? It worked yesterday!' (Dancing around the kitchen under the extractor fan kinda worked for a bit, if you want to try that.)

But a lot of the time nothing works. You try everything you can think of to soothe the cantankerous little honey badger in a babygrow.

For us, the witching hour almost always resulted in driving around in the car, working out how we were going to make the transfer from the car seat to the cot without waking her up…

… only for her to wake up as soon as we turned the engine off on the drive.

Just Stick to the Bloody Routine, Will You?!

You've finally got them in an evening routine that works. You dim the lights and have a relaxing little soak with some lovely lavender baby bath.

Wrapped in a fluffy soft towel with tinkly soothing music playing in the background, he has some yummy warm milk (not too warm, not too cold... just the right temperature), you do a little baby massage (just the way you learnt at that awful baby massage class you went to where he screamed his head off the whole time).

And then you gently place him in his cot, read a little story in a hushed voice and slowly inch away. His eyelids are definitely closing but you don't dare look at him, just in case…

And then…

Dad bursts into the room after coming home from work, picks him up for a cuddle and a tickle, and he's WIDE AWAKE!

Whatever Works

Spontaneity is no more; routine is your new best friend.

Before having a child, I was convinced I wouldn't be one of those mums obsessed by routine, but some days the routine is all that kept me sane.

My daughter loved knowing what was happening next and was a much happier baby once we'd got some kind of routine sorted.

Some parents are much more relaxed, and some are ruled by the clock. Whatever works!

We're all doing what we can to survive. Support your friends in their parenting choices, even if it's a completely different style to yours. You have no idea how much sleep she had last night or the battles she's facing to get through the day.

Pavement Pounding

Once you've worked out how to get your pushchair up without losing your shit, it'll be a godsend for getting your baby to sleep. (No guarantees. Don't send me hate mail if it doesn't work – all kiddos are different.)

To any new parent, naps are everything! The next time you see that mum or dad doing laps of the park with the pushchair muttering to themselves, make eye contact, give them a knowing smile. You understand that nap means so much.

Do Not Even Breathe!

You've spent the last hour shhhing, patting, humming and rocking... they're finally asleep! Yes! Hallelujah!!

Slowly, creep out of the room... shhh, shhh, creep, creep... Do not even breathe... DING DONG!! DING DONG!! Nooooooooooooooooooooo! Damn that fucking delivery driver!

People tell you to 'Make sure you make loads of noise around them from the start, so they get used to it.' Sure, some babies will sleep though anything, but others are such light sleepers they won't settle unless it's pretty much silent and there is no way you'd risk waking them up.

If you have one of these babies, make sure all phones are on silent, and maybe stick a polite note to the front door to warn visitors about the slumbering baby before you put them down for a nap.

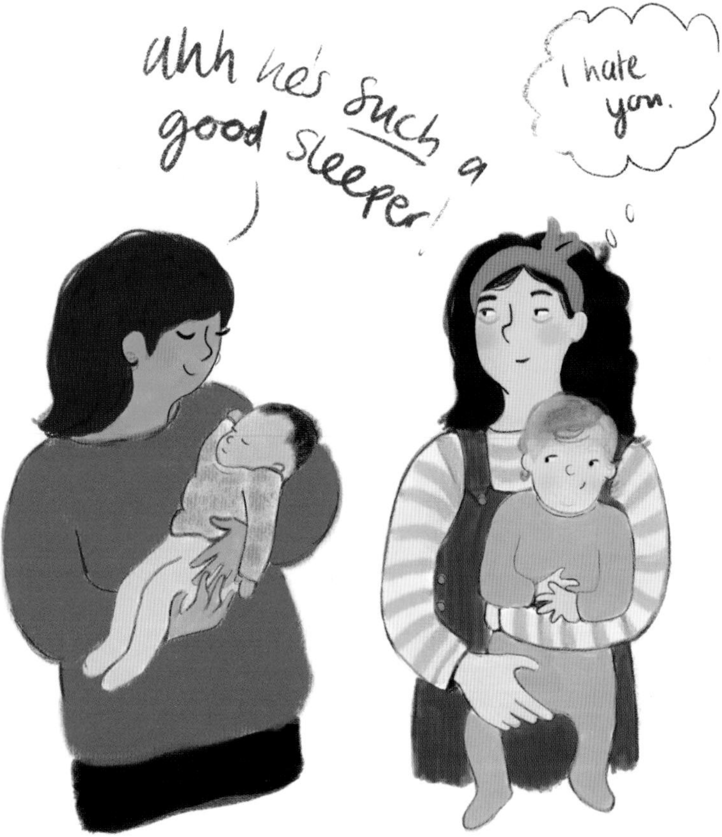
ahh he's such a good sleeper!
I hate you.

The Little Sleep Thief

Some babies sleep really well, some babies don't. If you're lucky enough to have one that does sleep well, be extra kind to your friends who have had about three seconds of unbroken sleep in the past four months.

Sleep deprivation (have I mentioned that before?) can be so, so tough. Everything can seem so much more overwhelming and desperate when you've had no sleep.

If you have a friend who has a baby that doesn't sleep, offer to come over and watch their baby while she has a much-needed nap or a bath.

Even a sympathetic text or FaceTime from a friend can make you feel less alone.

Five Things You'll Try to Get Your Baby to Sleep

1. Driving around the block 5000 times

zzzzzzzzz

shhhhhh

hmmmmm

brrrrmmm

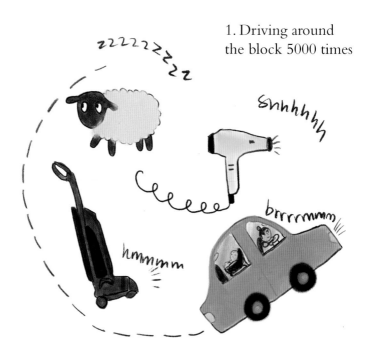

2. Hairdryers, hoovers, extractor fans, ANY white noise

3. Shhhing, patting, rocking, dancing, bopping

4. Buying multiple books on 'how to get your baby to sleep' but not having any time to read them

5. Lying on the floor holding tiny hands pretending to be asleep

Chapter 3
#mumlife

Finding Your People

Meeting other new mums and parents can be daunting, but it can also be incredibly supportive and comforting. Finding your 'mum crew' early on can be so important for your mental health, whether it's online, through NCT, baby groups, or chance meetings doing laps of the park with your pram.

These guys will become your guardian angels, saviours of sanity, fellow cake-scoffers, coffee-swiggers and, more importantly, a puke-stained shoulder to cry on.

Together you will navigate those early days of parenthood and excel in the art of one-handed eating and unfinished conversations.

Mothers' Meeting

Making new friends can be hard when you're an adult, especially when you've had no sleep and don't really feel like yourself.

Social anxiety and worrying what they'll think about your parenting skills (or lack of) can be a major barrier. Sometimes you just can't be arsed to put yourself 'out there'. After all, you may not have anything in common apart from the fact you have both reproduced.

But sometimes that's enough.

Just knowing that someone else is going through the same thing at the same time can be such a comfort. Having someone you can send a moany text to at 3 a.m. who will totally understand and who won't judge can make all the difference. Those small interactions can completely lift you up.

You might just meet a friend for life, but, if nothing else, it's a person who can hold your baby while you go and have a pee in peace.

Oh hi! I notice that you also wear dungarees and have bred we should be pals?

...OK

85

Ah yeah, Archie can sign 620 words now...

Comparison is the Thief of Joy

There's this thing that some mums do. They act like having a baby is part of a big fancy competition and you and your child are simply other contestants that they need to score points against.

- Is she crawling yet? Oh, mine started weeks ago!

- What percentile is yours on now?

- Can she say any words? Sleeping through? Is he good?

You know you shouldn't compare, but sometimes it's hard not to.

Some babies can walk before their first birthday, some don't even bother with the crawling stage and just drag their little bums along the floor in a strange crab-like manoeuvre, and, yes, some are fluent in Makaton by nine months. Try to remember, every single baby is an individual and they all meet milestones at different stages.

Spontaneous Combustion

Getting out of the house has now become a military operation.

Remember those days when you'd decide on the spur of the moment that you fancied a little wander around the shops? You'd grab your tiny handbag and skip out of the house in five minutes flat.

Yeah, those days are a distant memory – these days you'll pack for every single eventuality before you even start thinking about stepping out of your front door.

A change of clothes for them and you, another change of clothes just in case, more nappies than you need, all the wipes, milk, snacks, muslins, comforter, dummy, sling in case she won't go in the pushchair, pushchair in case she won't go in the sling. The list is endless…

The routine of getting out of the house can take a least an hour.

And nine times out of ten, just when you're finally ready to leave… hang on, what's that smell?

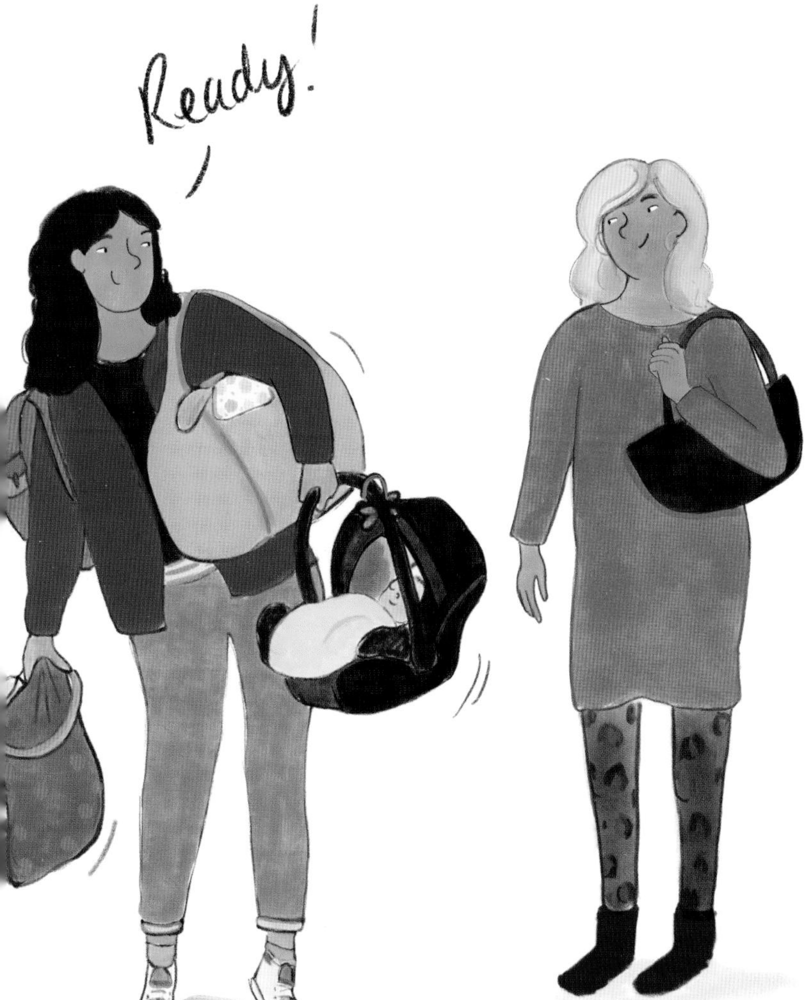
Ready!

hmm... did I lock the car?
oh poor her, I know how that feels.
agh, what do I d
this is so embarrass
I bet they think I
a crap mum...
Waaaah! waaaahhh!

Judgy Mums (Or Not)

Some mums are just dicks. They'll judge you to make themselves feel better and can be horrible and bitchy. Definitely avoid those mums. They were probably horrible humans before they had children.

But sometimes the judgement and criticism can be in your own head. You're so worried about getting things right you can forget that other parents probably haven't even noticed you, or how you're parenting, because they're too concerned they're being judged or are getting it wrong themselves.

The mental load of being a parent is huge. As a caregiver, you're always on high alert, always thinking about the next feed, nappy change, nap, mood, baby's needs as well as your own, combined with the normal responsibilities of being an adult.

Give yourself a break, we all have 'those days'.

Step Away From the App

When you don't know what you're doing, you can find yourself relying on advice from others to guide you. Some of the advice is really helpful, but there are so many apps, books, forums and online groups out there that a lot of the time it can become overwhelming.

You can become obsessed with the apps that tell you which 'shitstorm' is just around the corner and can prepare yourself for hurdles and phases that sometimes don't even happen with your baby. (And then you'll probably worry that it hasn't happened when the app said it should have.)

Take the advice on these platforms with a pinch of salt. Don't live by the 'what next?'

All babies are different.

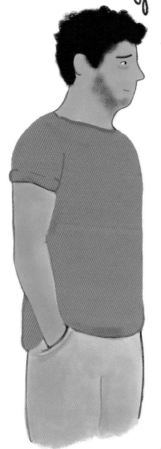

Oh crap! the app says she's going to start teething TONIGHT!!

Hating Mum and Baby Groups

For me, the thought of sitting in a village hall on a stained carpet with a bunch of strangers cooing like a group of overexcited pigeons, surrounded by grubby toys with snotty toddlers waddling about in bulging soggy nappies, is, quite frankly, the stuff of nightmares.

Group singing, going around the circle singing our babies' names and giving each other a foot massage, with the pungent aroma of baby shit, coffee and despair in the air, is just not something I enjoy.

Luckily for me, my child felt the same and would cry the whole time we were there, so after trying a couple of groups, we didn't return. And that was okay. Other things worked for us.

Did I have crippling 'mum guilt' about her not socialising with other babies and fear she'd not be able to make friends or become a normal functioning adult?

Yep, of course. See, I am a good mum.

Loving Mum and Baby Groups

However…

For former social butterflies, baby groups can be a lifeline, a break from the humdrum and essential for their mental health. Knowing that you have somewhere to go, something to fill your day with and the support of other parents is so important.

Happy parents = happy babies.

When you find a group of mums that 'get' you and you realise that you're not alone, hot tea, pink wafer biscuits and a good old moan can be a tonic!

Baby massage, daily drop-in centres, mum and baby yoga or messy play groups are all full of sleep-deprived mums looking for a friendly face.

Wherever you find your 'tribe', hang onto them with all your might, especially the ones who bake homemade brownies.

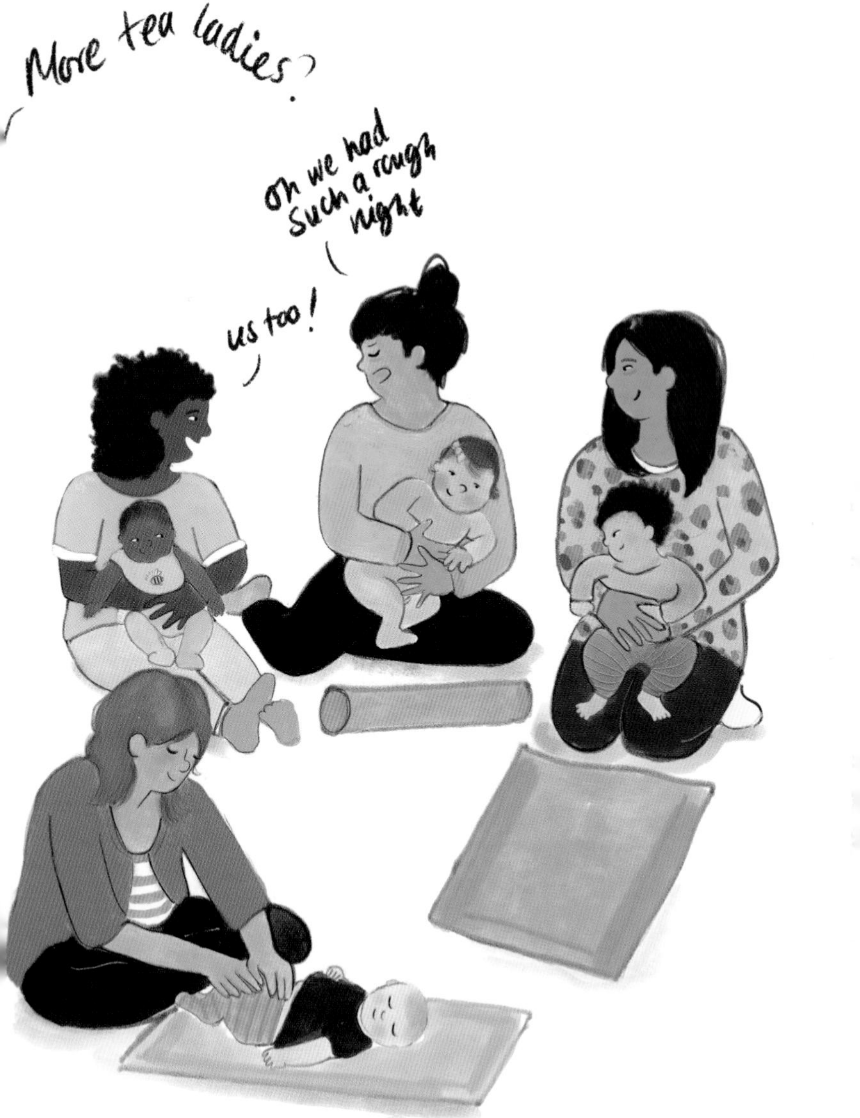
More tea ladies?
Oh we had such a rough night
us too!

She slept for 4 hours straight last night!
Wahooo!
Not happening tonight though Mum!

Don't Jinx It!

She slept for more than three hours straight!

Celebrate this momentous occasion with a friend. Treat yourself to a hot chocolate with extra marshmallows and a home foot spa.

You feel like a new woman, you have a spring in your step and are ready to take on the world! Even the bags under your eyes have faded a little!

Try to live in that moment.

Under no circumstances say any of the following: 'Ooh, have we turned a corner? Ahh great, that shows she can do it. Hope tonight will be the same. Right, now we need to work out exactly what we did last night and do exactly the same thing tonight – that'll work.'

Spoiler alert: it won't. It's a cruel trick.

Oversharing

The joy of meeting new mums in the same boat as you is that you can chat about literally anything birth or baby-related and they will be interested. (Do not try this with your child-free friends. They probably don't want to hear an in-depth description of your stitches or baby's cradle cap.)

With mums, conversation topics can go from gory birth stories to chat about green poo in an instant and your new pals won't even bat an eyelid. They will sympathise about your baby's constipation, offer tips that have worked for them and celebrate with you when your baby finally has that long-awaited dump.

You will wilfully send them photos of your C-section scar or a particularly weird poo (from the baby, not you… although…) and have group chats about leaking nipples and hairy chins. Cherish these newly found friendships. These ladies have seen you at your worst and still want to be friends. They've cried with you, laughed with you and know all your grossest secrets… The first rule of mum club: what's shared in the club, stays in the club, right?

Hot Tea and Sympathy

As a new mum, you'll find that sometimes the baby just won't be put down. Eating a meal, doing jobs around the house or putting a pushchair up all with one hand will be skills you master quicker than learning your ABCs at primary school.

One of the great things about meeting your mum crew in a café or coffee shop is that you can tag team! Hold each other's babies and take it in turns to drink hot tea like normal human beings.

When your support team aren't around, finding 'go-to' foods you can eat with one hand is always a good idea. Cake is great, biscuits, or fruit… nothing too fancy and definitely nothing that requires chopping up.

Adult Conversation

Never take for granted the time you managed to have a whole conversation with a friend or partner. Now you have a new conversation killer in the house, you'll appreciate those times even more.

After a few weeks of chatting to your new little crew member, you'll be desperate to have an adult conversation. Even the postman will be subjected to your ramblings.

When you finally do get to chat to a friend you will both talk non-stop. You're that happy to see another face the same size as yours, you'll start a hundred conversations and not finish any of them – in between feeding, burping and popping off to the loo to change bums, of course.

Although sometimes you'll be that exhausted, you'll both just sit there in silence, staring into space.

And that's just what you need.

I'm so tired I can't even string a sentence together...
I'm so glad we don't need to talk...

Five Things You Never Thought You'd Say to Someone You've Just Made Friends with... But Here We Are

Chapter 4
Is This Normal?

It's All a Phase

The moment you think you've got this parenting lark sussed, it'll all change. There will be another hurdle for you both to navigate and you'll be back at square one.

Sometimes it'll feel like you're never winning. The failsafe trick that's been working for the past few weeks is suddenly useless, and, as your baby graduates from the newborn phase, there are so many things awaiting them… and you.

Try to take each day as it comes and go with it. Next week there will no doubt be another thing you'll have to google two thousand times and pull your thinning hair out over.

Remember, this too shall pass. (Really fucking slowly and it'll feel like you're losing your mind, but, yep, it'll pass.)

Dr Google

What did parents do before the invention of Google?! Probably panicked a lot less, that's what!

If you rely on your phone to answer all of your baby-related questions, you're not alone…

- Baby won't sleep (589,000,000 results)

- Is my baby teething? (27,300,000 results)

- Why is my baby's poo a weird colour? (61,600,000 results)

You get the gist.

Sometimes you can go a bit Google crazy and it can make you even more anxious.

Always ask a health professional if you're worried — it's their job to help you.

Ignoring Sticky Beaks

Everyone will have an opinion on how to handle a certain phase your baby is going through: teething, weaning or sleeping (or not).

Learning to trust yourself is really hard, but you know your baby and what works for you. I may have said this already.

That busybody at the bus stop doesn't know that actually this is the first time you've made it out of the house all week. Or that you've been trying to persuade your baby to wear her coat for an hour before finally giving in and putting it in your bag. She doesn't know that you've been up all night with a grizzly teething baby and the only thing that soothes her is that blessed dummy.

Take a deep breath and bite your tongue.

You may not be aware, but as a new mum you have one free pass to tell a complete stranger to 'Fuck the fuck off' if they stick their nose in where it's not wanted. Use it wisely.

It's the Teeth

Teething is horrible.

Horrible for babies, horrible for parents, just horrible.

Teething makes everyone irritable, grumpy, despairing and generally fed up.

You'll try potions and powders, go through around fifteen dribble bibs a day, you'll even buy that ridiculously expensive bendy giraffe that you said you'd never buy. All in the desperate hope it'll ease the pain on their red-cheeked grizzly little face.

And you'll wish like nothing else that you could take that pain away from them.

However, the silver linings are 'He's teething' is a great excuse to not go on that playdate you've been dreading and you'll get lots more cuddles. When that bastard tooth finally makes an appearance, oh, the relief is momentous! Until the next one…

Prepare Yourself!

You've bought loads of recipe books, read all the advice and have been watching her like a hawk for the 'signs' that she's ready to start solids... You can't wait to get stuck in! The forums say it'll be enjoyable, show pictures of an apron-clad mum lovingly preparing homemade stews and peach compote.

Whether you choose baby-led weaning, whizzing up puree or bit of both, welcome to a whole new world of worry. For us, we did a bit of both. The baby-led weaning generally led to her gagging on a carrot baton or slice of toast and then me panicking that she was choking. Not the relaxing mealtimes I had in mind to be honest.

In hindsight, I probably felt a bit pressured to follow the latest trend and once we'd got into our own way of doing things it was much less stressful.

Oh, and nobody mentions the nappies that will follow that meal. Brace, brace, brace!

Food Critic

Voila! A homemade delight, made with loads of good stuff, packed with vitamins… she's going to love this. I'm such a good mum, look at me! I've even made an extra one for the freezer…

Don't take it personally if your baby spits out the food that you have just taken over an hour to prepare. Apparently, you need to offer the same food at least eight times before they decide that they fucking hate your cooking.

Smush

Remember before you had your own baby and friends and family would send you pictures of their little cherub covered head to toe in green mush or pasta sauce, and, be honest, you thought, 'Eww that's gross and quite frankly a bit weird.'

Look at you now.

'Ahhh, look he's got avocado in his eyebrows – quick! Let's send a picture to the family WhatsApp group.'

Before you start a mealtime, make sure you prepare the area like you're about to perform a forensic investigation: cover the floor with a plastic sheet, dress the child in the biggest waterproof bib you can find… and try your hardest to relax. This is going to get messy, go with it.

My top tips would be:

Choose a practical, easy-to-clean high chair. It won't be the prettiest but you'll be glad you did.

Don't forget to check behind their ears and in their neck creases at bath time.

Floor Food

The general advice says you should sterilise baby stuff for at least a year. The advice doesn't mention the fact that babies will crawl along the floor and eat the cat's dinner, bits of fluff, crumbs, and even woodlice.

This is all normal behaviour; babies won't always eat your cooking, but they will happily munch on a dusty four-week-old biscuit they find under the sofa, handfuls of sand on the beach and leaves in the park. Try not to worry too much. What goes in usually comes out in their next nappy.

My friend's baby once chewed on a glittery Christmas card and produced a very sparkly Christmas turd. It certainly made changing stinky nappies more interesting!

ba ba ba ba
Oh my god Mum, did you hear that?! I think she might be gifted!

Genius

'He's definitely gifted – did you see him do that?!'
'Oh my god, do you think we should reserve him a place at that posh school now?'

Everyone thinks their baby is a genius. They grow and change so much so quickly that when they can do new things that they couldn't do yesterday it can blow your mind.

Sometimes it can be just like watching a little science experiment. You can tell when paths and bits 'n' bobs (technical term) have connected in their tiny brains. Seeing them discover they can do new things is magical!

Babies are fascinating to watch, which is a good job, as you can lose days just staring at them.

So Many Toys

It is a fact that the more toys you buy them, the more they'll want to play with a saucepan or happily just sit in a cardboard box.

You'll spend hours researching the 'best educational toys' that will help their development, spend half your maternity pay on the latest wooden toys and gadgets, and their favourite thing to play with will be your keys.

Save your money and just buy a spare TV control, or a few extra wooden spoons.

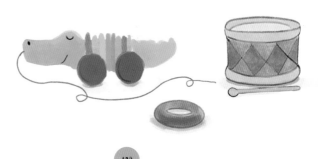

expensive wooden toys

Most favourite thing ever

On the Move

One minute they'll be sitting just there where you left them… and the next minute they've commando-rolled out of the room and are sat in the garden picking up ants and eating them.

Shit just got real. They're on the move. You'll need to have eyes in the back of your head now. That's it – no going back!

Don't get cocky – make sure you have baby proofed the house weeks before they show signs of planning their escape, the front door is locked, the stair gate is shut and anything precious is out of reach.

If you need to get stuff done or fancy having a wee on your own, then make sure you get a play pen (aka baby jail).

Personal Space – What's That?

Say hello to your new little bathroom buddy, toilet companion and invader of personal space.

Never again will you have a poo in peace. Once they can crawl, you'll either be followed around the house, or you won't trust them not to wreck the place or hurt themselves in the three seconds it takes you to have a quick wee.

Your cute little stalker will even accompany you to have a shower, point at your overgrown bush and giggle. Body shamed by a baby, oh the irony.

You can trust that they'll wait until you've lathered up your hair with shampoo before they grab the loo roll and decorate the bathroom, or decide that they fancy smearing a whole tub of nappy cream into their hair.

The alternative is to put the baby safely in a play pen and have the quickest shower ever while you hear imaginary cries coming from the other room.

Karma (Sorry, Mum)

Before having a baby, you kind of assume that they're all the same, and for a while it's true. All they do is eat, poo, cry, and sleep (or not). But slowly their little personalities start to emerge and it's then that you realise you have created a cantankerous, opinionated mini version of yourself.

Sweet old ladies in cafés will tell you your baby is 'spirited' or kindly remind you that 'You've got your hands full with that one.'

You'll probably have days when everything just goes to shit, usually when you've planned to have a really lovely day out. Teething, a development stage or just a tired baby who's not up for socialising can make you abandon all plans and run for home.

Have low expectations and accept that some days will just be a complete shitshow.

Potty Mouth

For the first couple of months of parenthood, you can curse to your heart's delight and get away with it. After that, you should probably rein it in a little, unless you want their first words to be 'twat' or 'fuck it'.

You may not realise it, but babies are ALWAYS listening, taking it all in, connecting all the dots, and they will most definitely repeat what they hear at the most embarrassing moment possible.

Also be careful what you say about your mother-in-law, especially if she spends lots of time with your baby. There is now an undercover parrot behind enemy lines.

Can you believe she used to be this small?!
She'll be a toddler soon!

Let It Go

Letting go of the newborn phase can be really emotional. Packing away those teeny-tiny little vests and socks that no longer fit can turn you into a blubbering wreck.

It's a big deal, especially if you're not having any more babies.

Carefully fold up that tiny little outfit you brought them home in on that first day and marvel at how far you've both come!

They grow so quickly and you'll squeeze them into that favourite little vest that makes them look so cute for as long as possible, but at some point you're going to have to get rid of the bags of tiny baby clothes. Do not squirrel them away into the loft to gather dust. Keep a couple of the special outfits but try to pass the ones without shit stains on to an expectant mum (if she can prise them out of your iron grip).

Bribery and Corruption

Bribing them with snacks, screens, or a new toy is standard procedure. Don't feel bad, we all do it and most of the time it works like a treat!

You'll drill it into them to 'share, share, share', that 'sharing is caring', to use 'kind hands' and 'be nice' – and they'll probably ignore you, which is ironic as you'll have to share your bed, personal space, partner and body parts with them from the moment they open their eyes.

The one thing you can guarantee that they'll share with you is their snotty germs, especially when they sneeze directly into your eyeballs. Oh the joys!

Five Essential Things You'll Need to Take with You Every Time You Even Think About Leaving the House

1. Snacks for you both – you need to keep your strength up

2. Two more nappies than you think you'll need

3. The baby (easily done, no judgement here!)

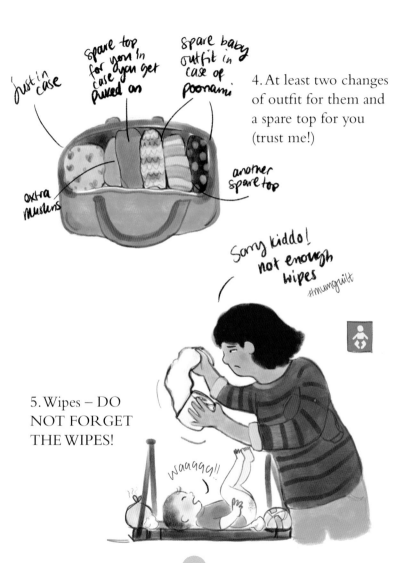

just in case

spare top for you in case you get puked on

spare baby outfit in case of poonami

4. At least two changes of outfit for them and a spare top for you (trust me!)

another spare top

extra muslins

Sorry kiddo! not enough wipes #mumguilt

5. Wipes – DO NOT FORGET THE WIPES!

waaaaa!!

Chapter 5
A Brand-New You

Same, Same (But Different)

Let's be real: motherhood is an absolute rollercoaster, whether or not you feel like you bossed it from the get-go, or are still feeling like you're just about surviving it. It's okay to grieve for your old life (oh, Saturday lie-in, how I miss you!) and it's okay to admit you're finding it really hard. It IS hard!

Some days will feel like you're facing a mountain you don't have the energy to climb. You'll drag your ass to the end of the day, knowing that the night is going to be just as hard.

Make sure you look after yourself too. In fact, it is essential. Take any help that's offered: a 10-minute nap, a chapter of a book, or a soak in the bath can make you feel like you've had a mini spa break.

Somehow, you will get to a place where a new you will emerge. Yes, you're knackered, and you still have a little cry whilst doing the dishes, but you're okay with it. This is a new you: good, bad, ugly crying and all.

Human Beans

When you think about it, the whole concept is completely mind-blowing, isn't it? A whole human being with a personality and dreams and limbs and everything, growing inside the body of another human... What the hell?!

This is without doubt your biggest achievement and you should be so, so proud of yourself. You grew an awesome little person – the sky's the limit!

The 'Just had a Baby' Pants

Before your baby arrived, you bought a few pairs of those huge comfy granny pants, just to wear for that gross bit in the first few weeks where you bleed and sweat and generally feel yucky. (If you don't know about that bit then you should definitely be googling that shit.)

You purchase the giant undercrackers thinking that you'll just wear them for a bit, temporary residents in the knicker drawer as it were, definitely not for the future, just for now… but then…

Ohhh, how amazing are they?!

Like a comforting hot water bottle hugging your tum, so reliable, dependable and practical, these beauties will never let you down by giving you a wedgy or digging in. They love comfort food, second helpings and are perfect for tucking that post-preggo tummy into.

Fuck it, there's no going back now.

151

We're Freeeeeeeeeee!

You've finally arranged for a babysitter to come over so you can go for that long-awaited meal out. You both really need to remember that you actually liked each other once, that you are more than just 'Mummy and Daddy'.

So you start the bedtime routine at 5 p.m. If this is going to work it needs to be run like a military operation. You write down a list for the babysitter of 'things to try' if she wakes up, squeeze yourself into that top that used to fit, even wear your favourite jewellery for the first time in ages.

Yes, she's asleep, we can go…

That moment when you both get out of the house is pure bliss, you're like a pair of excitable cocker spaniels going out on a walk.

However, don't be surprised if once the excitement has worn off, you spend 90 percent of the evening talking about your kid, scrolling through pictures of the baby on your phone, before going home early because you both miss her. Magic.

You Do You

It took me a long time to realise that you don't have to do things the way everyone else does. You don't have to take them to baby swimming at three months old if you don't feel comfortable doing that. If you want to teach them baby sign language, that's great. Or don't.

Doing things your own way and not following the crowd will not make you a bad parent and your confidence will definitely grow over time.

Motherhood will present you with a plethora of opportunities to feel the dreaded 'mum guilt', but as a general rule, if you're happy then the chances are your baby will be too.

By looking after your own mental health, you'll be the best mum that you can be.

This is so not me..
Why am I here?!
I should have just had a coffee while she napped
Waaaaaa!!

does he look pale? is he ill? I think he's ill..

No Mum, he fine, Just needs a poo.

Intuition

Before you have a baby, people will tell you to 'trust your instincts' and you'll be pretty much clueless about what that actually means. You'll worry that you won't have any instincts... or stress that they won't 'work'.

But the reality is that mums have a superpower. Some call it instincts, some call it a funny feeling, but it's actually just some dark kind of witchy magic – you just know when something doesn't feel right. By the time you're a few months in, you know them so well you can tell from one ear grab that they need a nap or that they feel tired or just not themselves. You even know their bowel habits better than you know your own.

This small person is a part of you – you are all they have ever known. It makes sense that you have a crazy connection. Even if it takes a while to trust yourself, you will get there.

You have survived for nearly a whole year. Celebrate that achievement! Buy yourself something nice or have a child-free coffee date with a pal.

All Change

Sometimes you won't recognise yourself, this new version of you, sticking to a routine, being a grown-up, keeping another human alive… and actually doing okay.

You see that wonderful little human being with chubby butter rolls for thighs, giggling at his own reflection. You made that.

You are more than enough.

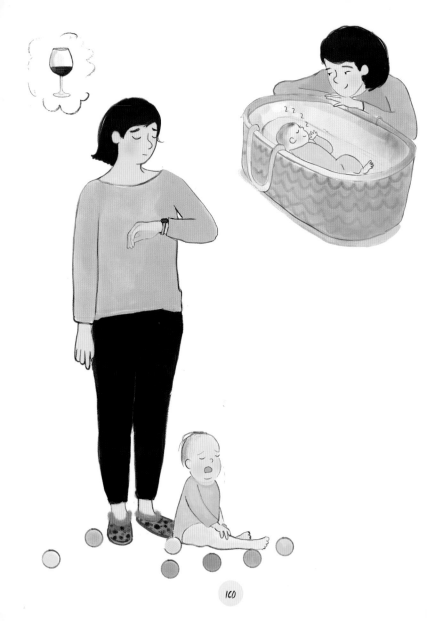

But Sometimes…

Babies are really fucking annoying.

Some days, they'll push you to your absolute limits – you'll count down the minutes until bedtime, when hopefully you get to 'relax' and have some 'me time' for a bit.

Parenting can be relentless, physically and mentally exhausting, and by the end of the day you'll be running on empty and just want silence… or to watch a bloody TV programme that's not for kids.

But the even more annoying thing is that when they're asleep, you kind of miss them…! What's that all about?

Stop Growing – It's Going Too Quickly!

You won't believe how fast time goes. Everyone will say to you 'Oh enjoy every second.' And you'll think, 'Oh bugger off, as if I can enjoy every second!' Even the seconds when they're screaming for hours? Or puking all over your hair that you've just washed for the first time in weeks, or refusing to take that nap that you both so desperately need?

Looking back, I do feel bad that I didn't 'enjoy' it more, but that's so easy to say in hindsight. Don't beat yourself up if you're really not enjoying it. You are surviving.

Sorry to say but the cliché is right: the days can be so long… but the years will fly!

. . . "this is so hard, I can't wait until she's a bit bigger..."

agh! where has my baby gone.?? please stop growing so fast!

Ah, mat leave must be like one long holiday, right?

yeah I think so...

. learn spanish,
.. write my novel,
.. learn to crochet..
..maybe start a business

Plans Plans
, Plans...

Most of my
← time

Thwarted Plans

If, like me, you had so many plans for your maternity leave – plans to learn a new language, declutter the house or even to start a new little business – and all those plans went to shit the moment the baby arrived, then don't worry, you're not alone.

Some mums manage to do all of those amazing things and more, and others spend 90 percent of their time trapped under a baby who won't sleep anywhere but nestled into their neck.

If all you've achieved on your maternity leave is getting through each day, and if everyone is fed and happy, then that's enough.

I wouldn't have spent mine any other way, shitty nappies and all.

Unexpected Visitors

You had an absolutely terrible night, and the house looks like a bomb has just gone off. There's a rank pile of dirty nappies bulging out of a ridiculously small nappy bin in the corner and dirty washing is piled up everywhere. (You would tidy up but, seriously, what's the point? It'll be a mess again in about ten minutes!)

You walk past the hallway mirror and your own reflection actually startles you for a second. 'Is that really me?!' You look like you've been dragged through a hedge, with huge dark circles under your eyes and newly-formed wrinkles you swear weren't there yesterday. There's also a faint aroma of baby vomit and stale milk following you around.

No, today you're both going to hibernate and fester in your pit.

Today you do not want to see anyone. You want to just get through the day in your PJs and hide from the world.

Mark my words, this will be the day your only childfree friend pops over unannounced to see the baby and have a natter.

oh crap! there's NO way i'm letting her see this shit tip!
oh hiya I was just passing!

Besotted

It really is a love like no other. You can't describe how much you love them…

Just your own kid, mind. Other people's children are still really fucking annoying.

I naively assumed that once I became a mother myself, I'd turn into Mary Poppins and naturally adore all babies and children.

It turns out that even though I am besotted with my own, I still think other people's kids are annoying little pricks.

You've Survived!

There are so many 'ways to parent' these days. The pressure can be overwhelming. The trying to do it all, still having a successful career, doing the things that make you *you* and being the perfect mum is exhausting.

Society expects mums to work like they don't have children and have children like they don't work. Hopefully, one day that will change, but right now you're doing your best and that is good enough.

In this online world we find ourselves living in, social media can make you feel inadequate. It can feel like all the other mums have got their shit together and are crafting and baking vegan sugar-free cookies, whilst you're barely managing to have a shower and shave your pits. Rest assured that most of it is not real life and behind every Instaworthy shot is a mum scratching baby puke off her shoulder or putting on extra concealer to cover how tired she looks.

There will be lots of things you may not enjoy about being a new mum and that's totally normal. The best part is your offspring will think you are amazing, no matter what.

Five Things You Won't Believe

1. How little sleep you actually need

2. That you'd do anything to make them happy

3. How many times you can try unsuccessfully to leave the house

Oh ffs! I've forgotten the wipes!

I love being your mum

4. How much you love them

5. How fast it goes... WTF how is she one already?!

You Did It!

You survived the newborn stage, the sleepless nights (sorry, there will be a few more of those to come), and that phase you thought would never end and had you obsessively googling at 2 a.m. Despite the challenges you had to push through and the struggles you faced, you did it! You've even finally worked out how to put the pushchair up with one hand!

They said it would get easier and it kind of did. Or did you just get used to it?

Hopefully, by now you are feeling a bit more like yourself and the baby brain isn't too bad. I honestly think it took me at least a couple of years before my brain started working again (zero sleep will do that to you), and even now I feel forever changed. Not better, not worse, just different.

The toddler years are on the horizon, and although some of the rumours are true – they are a whole new level of crazy – they are definitely not boring!

But, for now, just take a moment to enjoy your glory. You made it! A whole year of being a mum, can you believe it?! Now go and make yourself a nice cup of tea to celebrate. Just don't expect to drink it whilst it's hot!

THE

ILLUSTRATOR

—